TREE FROGS

by Jaclyn Jaycox

PEBBLE
a capstone imprint

Pebble Explore is published by Pebble, an imprint of Capstone.
1710 Roe Crest Drive
North Mankato, Minnesota 56003
www.capstonepub.com

Library of Congress Cataloging-in-Publication Data
Names: Jaycox, Jaclyn, 1983- author.
Title: Tree frogs / by Jaclyn Jaycox.
Description: North Mankato, Minnesota : Pebble, [2021] | Series: Animals | Includes bibliographical references and index. | Audience: Ages 5-8 | Audience: Grades 2-3 | Summary: "There are more than 800 kinds of tree frogs. Some of them don't even live in trees! But they all have very unusual feet. Find out more about this large family of frogs"— Provided by publisher.
Identifiers: LCCN 2021002477 (print) | LCCN 2021002478 (ebook) | ISBN 9781977132024 (hardcover) | ISBN 9781977133045 (paperback) | ISBN 9781977155177 (pdf) | ISBN 9781977156792 (kindle edition)
Subjects: LCSH: Hylidae—Juvenile literature.
Classification: LCC QL668.E24 J39 2021 (print) | LCC QL668.E24 (ebook) | DDC 597.8/78—dc23
LC record available at https://lccn.loc.gov/2021002477
LC ebook record available at https://lccn.loc.gov/2021002478

Image Credits
Alamy: F. Rauschenbach, 17; Capstone Press, 6; Shutterstock: CanuckStock, 12, Charles Bergman, 11, COULANGES, 21, Daniel Pask, 24, Dirk Ercken, Cover, Heiko Kiera, 15, Kurit afshen, 1, 5, 13, 25, LM Photos, 9, Louis.Roth, 18, Luis Louro, 7, Peter Reijners, 14, phdwhite, 27, QuickStartProjects, 22, Rich Carey, 28, StevenThomasPhotography, 19, worldswildlifewonders, 10

Editorial Credits
Editor: Hank Musolf; Designer: Dina Her; Media Researcher: Morgan Walters; Production Specialist: Tori Abraham

All internet sites appearing in back matter were available and accurate when this book was sent to press.

Table of Contents

Words in **bold** are in the glossary.

Amazing Tree Frogs

Hop! Hop! What is that jumping from branch to branch? A tree frog! These animals may be small, but they take big jumps. Some of these frogs can jump 50 times their body length!

Tree frogs are a type of **amphibian**. They live in the water when they are young. They can live on land or in water as adults.

Tree frogs are different from other frogs. They are smaller. They also have sticky toes that cling to trees. There are more than 800 kinds of tree frogs.

Where in the World

Tree frogs live on every **continent** except Antarctica. More than 600 kinds can be found in South and Central America alone. Most types of tree frogs live in trees.

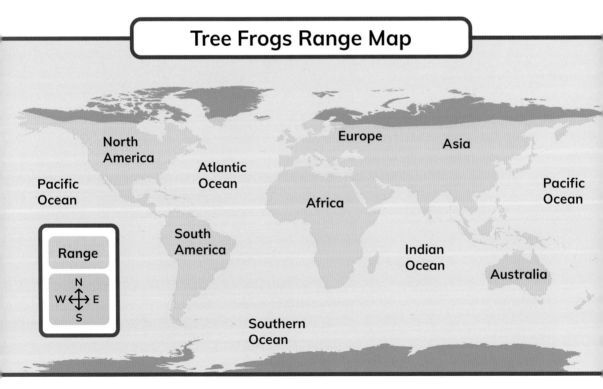

Tree Frogs Range Map

Some live on the ground. They can live in ponds or lakes. They live in grasslands and marshes too.

Tree frogs are **cold-blooded**. If it's hot outside, they are hot. If it's cold outside, they are cold.

Most tree frogs live in warm, tropical areas. If it gets too hot, they hide in hollow trees or under tree bark to cool down.

Some tree frogs live where it's cold. Gray tree frogs spend winters under dead leaves. Their bodies actually freeze. Their hearts stop beating. In the spring, they warm up and start living normally again.

gray tree frog

Tiny Tree Frogs

Tree frogs can be many different colors. Many are brown, green, or gray. Their colors help them blend in with their surroundings. Some tree frogs even change color. White's tree frogs can change from bright green to bluish purple.

red-eyed tree frog

poison dart frogs

Poisonous tree frogs are more colorful. Poison dart frogs can be blue, yellow, and orange. Their bright colors tell **predators** to stay away.

Pacific tree frog on blade of grass

Tree frogs can be many different sizes. But most are very small. They have to be light enough for small branches to hold them.

White-lipped tree frogs are the biggest in the world. They can grow up to 5.5 inches (14 centimeters) long. That's still shorter than a pencil.

Some of the smallest tree frogs are less than 1 inch (2.5 cm) long. That's about the size of a grape!

white-lipped tree frog

Tree frogs have thin bodies. They have long legs. They have special pads on their fingers and toes. The pads are sticky. They help them to climb trees. Their toes are also very bendy. It helps them grip leaves and branches.

a red-eyed tree frog climbing a plant

red-eyed tree frog

Most tree frogs have large, dark eyes. Some have gold specks. The red-eyed tree frog has bright red eyes. It stays hidden under leaves. When it is threatened, it opens its eyes. The color can scare predators away.

On the Menu

A tree frog sits and waits. Soon, a bug buzzes nearby. The frog opens its mouth. It shoots out its long, sticky tongue and grabs the bug. The frog has caught its dinner!

Tree frogs eat plants when they are young. When they are adults, they eat insects. They eat ants, crickets, and moths. They eat beetles and flies too. Some bigger tree frogs may even eat mice.

Tree frogs don't chew their food.
They swallow it whole. The frogs use
their eyes to help. When they blink, it
pushes their food down.

Tree frogs usually hunt at night. They sleep during the day. They can see better at night than most other animals in the world. They can even see color in darkness!

Life of a Tree Frog

Tree frogs usually live alone. They only come together to **mate**. Males make croaking sounds to attract females. The sounds also warn other males to stay away.

Tree frogs lay eggs. A group of eggs is called a clutch. The average clutch size is about 50 eggs. But some frogs can lay up to 4,000 eggs. Most eggs take less than a week to hatch.

a red-eyed tree frog and her eggs

a tree frog tadpole

Most tree frogs lay their eggs in water. Some lay them on leaves that hang over the water. When the eggs hatch, the babies fall into the water below. The mother and father usually don't stay with the eggs. Many eggs are eaten by predators.

Baby tree frogs are called tadpoles. They have tails. They eat small plants called **algae**. Tree frogs live in the water as they grow. Their tails start to disappear. They grow legs.

When tadpoles become adult frogs, they leave the water. They can breathe air. Some types of tree frogs become adults in just a few weeks. For others, it can take many months.

Australian white tree frog

The life span is different for each kind of tree frog. Some live only about one year. But others can live much longer. The Australian tree frog lives up to 15 years.

Dangers to Tree Frogs

Tree frogs have a lot of predators. Birds, bats, and snakes eat tree frogs. Squirrels and raccoons do too. Fish eat tree frog tadpoles.

Disease is also a threat to tree frogs. Many have died from a **fungus** that lives in the water. Tree frogs breathe through their skin. This disease affects their skin and makes it hard for them to breathe.

Taiwain whistling thrushes eat frogs.

Humans are also a danger to tree frogs. Many tree frogs live in rain forests. People are cutting down these forests. They are using the land for farming. Tree frogs are losing their homes.

The number of some kinds of tree frogs is going down. But groups of people are trying to help them. They are working to protect the land they live on.

Fast Facts

Name: tree frog

Habitat: tropical rain forests, grasslands, marshes, ponds, lakes

Where in the World: every continent except Antarctica

Food: insects, mice

Predators: fish, birds, bats, snakes, squirrels, raccoons, humans

Life span: average of 5 years

Glossary

algae (AL-jee)—small plants without roots or stems that grow in water

amphibian (am-FI-bee-uhn)—an animal that lives in the water when it is young and on land as an adult; some amphibians, such as frogs, can live both in the water and on land as adults

cold-blooded (KOHLD-BLUHD-id)—having a body temperature that changes with the surrounding temperature

continent (KAHN-tuh-nuhnt)—one of Earth's seven large land masses

fungus (FUHN-guhs)—a living thing similar to a plant, but without flowers, leaves, or green coloring

mate (MATE)—to join with another to produce young

poisonous (POI-zuhn-uhss)—able to harm or kill with poison or venom

predator (PRED-uh-tur)—an animal that hunts other animals for food

Read More

Amstutz, Lisa J. *F is for Frogs: ABCs of Endangered Amphibians*. North Mankato, MN: Capstone Press, 2017.

Donohue, Moira Rose. *Tree Frogs: Life in the Leaves*. New York: Scholastic, Inc., 2020.

Golkar, Golriz. *Red-Eyed Tree Frogs*. Minneapolis: Pop!, 2019.

Internet Sites

Active Wild–Red-Eyed Tree Frog Facts
activewild.com/red-eyed-tree-frog-facts/

Fort Wayne Children's Zoo–Orange-Eyed Tree Frogs
kidszoo.org/our-animals/orange-eyed-tree-frog/

National Geographic Kids–Red-Eyed Tree Frog
kids.nationalgeographic.com/animals/amphibians/
red-eyed-tree-frog/

Index